ANOINTING HIS WORD AND PRAISE

Without Knowing God Was Really There

VOL. 5

with

REV. OSCAR DIXON

© Copyright 2021 by Oscar Dixon, Sr

PRAYERS by FIRST EDITION: SCRIPTURES AND COMMENTARIES:

New International Version King James Version Strong Exhaustive Concordance Word Study New Statement Word Study Dictionary Thayer's Greek

All rights reserved. No parts of this book may be reproduced in any form without permission in writing from the publisher, writer, and editor.

All rights reserved. No parts of this book may be reproduced in any form without permission in writing from the publisher, writer, and editor.

No part of this publication may be reproduced, stored in a retrial system, or transmitted in any form or by any means or electronics, mechanical, photo-copy, recording, or otherwise without prior consent or permission focus on the family.

ISBN: 978-1-943409-87-7

All Rights Reserved

Table of Contents

PART I ANOINTING

Chapter One 8
  KEEP PRAYING
Chapter Two 13
  LORD GROW MY OFFICE
Chapter Three 17
  GOD WONDERS NEVER CEASE II
Chapter Four 21
  HE GROWS US
Chapter Five 25
  TRUST, HAVE PATIENCE
Chapter Six 32
  A ROD AND STAFF
Chapter Seven 37
  THUS, SAYS THE LORD

PART II HIS WORD

Chapter One 42
  MESSAGES IN OUR DREAMS I
Chapter Two 47
  MESSAGES IN OUR DREAMS II
Chapter Three 51
  HE SENDS A WORD
Chapter Four 56
  ALWAYS PRAY
Chapter Five 61
  RESTORATION

Chapter Six 68
    FOR A MOMENT; HE HID HIS ANGER

Chapter Seven 75
    RAISE YOUR STAFF

Chapter Eight 81
    STAND IN THE KITCHEN

Chapter Nine 86
    GOD MAKES PROPHETS

PART III PRAISE

Chapter One 91
    HE IS PREPARING US

Chapter Two 95
    YOU NEED TO STAND

Chapter Three 99
    DECLARE THE WORKS OF GOD

Chapter Four 102
    PRAISE HIM

Chapter Five 107
    LEARNING OBEDIENCE

DEDICATION

Rev. Frank D. Dixon Mrs. Ethel M. Dixon

During my youth, I don't remember home life with an uncomfortable lifestyle; our parents had a harmonious relationship. I don't remember loud boisterous voices and disagreements coming through the house in the midst of seven children.

My innocence betrayed me as I grew older. What I was experiencing was not the norm in other homes; we had hard times, shortages of everything, but the love of our parents for us and the Lord, words can't describe.

My dad and mother were always hugging and playing with us. I didn't know it then, but there were spiritual blessings of impartation placed on our lives. We grew up; passing on to our children what we received from our parents; the Lord of their lives, is the Lord of our lives. We believe the Lord brought our parents up the rough side of the mountain and set them on a solid foundation in Christ Jesus the Solid Rock; and so, it is with us. I also dedicate these writings and testimonies to our parents, sisters and brothers; and to all our children and family members both near and far. They are to tell the story, it will to be in concert with our upbringing, it is our legacy why we serve the Lord.

ANOINTING HIS WORD AND PRAISE

Vol. 6, 7 and 8

Chapter One

KEEP PRAYING

Ephesian 3:16: That He would grant you, according to the riches of his glory to be strengthened with might by His Spirit in the inner man.

"Hello Oscar, I'm sending this note to you because I need prayer. There is so much happening to me right now. I am trying to survive a turn of events, but it is more than I can manage, even with the help of my family and others. I know all families have disagreements and fallouts.

Somewhere along the way we learn to walk away from our disagreements and begin again. We pray forgiveness and apologize to one another and all is well. This time it doesn't feel right because there doesn't seem to be any healing and cleansing coming. Everyone seems very set in their position and acting unlovable." Family, those that read this journal and can identify with issues within your family that have brought separation with attitudes that keep us from loving one another; be not deceived. We aren't able of ourselves to turn love and caring affection back into the family again. We can't know the depth of the individuals fall-out. We, in ourselves, can't know how deep and how long this void has been deteriorating in our family. I urge each of us too give ourselves and our families to the Lord. Only the Lord is able to look at our heart and declare what must be done to heal our wounded spirit and make us whole again.

In fact, it's His job to keep you whole, so you can get away from the non-essentials that don't benefit you or your circumstances. The Lord wants us to be encouraged, have faith and believe that what we prayed for will be done according to His will. Hit the side- walk and tell somebody that Jesus wants to be Lord over our lives and He has purposed each of us to be a disciple for Him from the beginning.

My friend who wrote me the message in the opening of this chapter, reminded me that we discovered each other some time ago through our e-mails and we renewed our relationship. She said, "I remembered you are a man of faith and you have prayed for me in the past and once again I am asking you to pray and "Keep Praying," for our family, jobs, and myself. I believe you are a humble man and the Lord hears your prayers. Your name did come into my spirit and I hastened to send you the note asking for support in our difficult time."

We all must remember the Lord will answer our prayer "if it's in His will." When I received that note, I immediately went to my knees in prayer and sent a fresh anointing of the Holy Spirit to cover and comfort her and the family. I prayed to send the Lord's angels around her and the household during their time of loss. I asked our Father to help with the challenges to come.

There was a time in the "Night Watch," I had been praying to the Lord to help me pray and speak His words to others, so they will know and believe they have heard from the Most Highest. It was early in the night when I heard this powerful comment come into my spirit. I heard the Lord say, "Stand on my Word." Then I saw the Holy Bible pass before me and the statement was still resounding within my spirit.

I decided to whole my piece shut until the Lord give me a word to share with the family; this way I can wait on His Word myself.

Please remember our Lord has a beauty in Him that nothing and no one can surpass. He stands by His word. He doesn't say something and hide His hand like our fellow man, brothers and sisters. When we have disagreements in the family, it doesn't matter what the reason is, take it to the Lord in prayer. Petition His divine intervention and develop a bulldog bite. Don't let go until you hear from heaven with saving grace and mercy from our Lord and Savior, Jesus Christ.

Remember to "Keep Praying," and believing that your righteous prayers to our Lord will touch His spirit and bring Him into your situation. He doesn't ask us to beg Him but to come with Thanksgiving, Praise and Worship to the Lord of all.

Watch your mountains become mole-hills. Your sleepless nights will turn into wonderful visions as you remember how the Lord showered His grace on you.

TRANSLATION: Ephesian 3:16:

Let Christ dwell in my heart by faith, and let me be rooted and ground in love, and let me comprehend with all saints what is the breadth and length and depth and height of your love.

Chapter Two

LORD GROW MY OFFICE

*Ephesians 1:18 (NIV) I pray also that the eyes of your heart may be enlightened in order that you may know the hope to which he has
called you, the riches of his glorious inheritance in the saints.*

I met a young doctor through a very trusted friend. She suggested that I make an appointment to see him and that he was and extraordinary person and doctor. He teaches a natural path of healthy choices for wellness. She had been treated by this doctor and he discovered issues that needed immediate care.

These areas had not been noted by her previous doctor and they were of serious concern.

As she and I talked, I felt The Holy Spirit. I said, "Make me and appointment; whatever it is, I'll accept it." This was a Monday afternoon. She called me back shortly thereafter. My appointment was made for the next day at 1:00 pm.

I was thoroughly surprised, so I asked her, "What did you say to the doctor?" She said, "I told him, "You need to meet Oscar."

I discovered later that the doctor canceled previous appointments to make time for me. We often say, "that's God's favor". As it turned out, God's intention was to address some situations and circumstances that the doctor was facing.

Our first visit was very helpful. I believe, from a vision I had a few days before, that I was led to him through my friend. This was the Lord extending His mighty hand to bring help when needed.

Whenever I am going to an engagement of any sort, I always invite the Holy Spirit to come and be with me, so that I may understand things that I ordinarily wouldn't understand.

On my second visit, my friend mentioned to me that the doctor was considering adding additional work to his practice. She told him to "tell Oscar". He asked why, and she told him that she just thinks he ought to.

Their conversation was that Sunday and my appointment was Tuesday. I had a powerful session with the doctor. He needed to take some time to prepare a prescription for me. It would need to be filled soon so I told him I'll come back the following morning to pick it up.

There was more to my visit than picking up my prescription. When I arrived, we began to talk. Through our conversation, he shared with me that he started his herbal product line and was stocking it on the shelves. At that time, I was prompted by the Holy Spirit to pray for him and anoint his hands to do the work that was already in his heart to do. The Anointing that came was an awesome presence from the Holy Spirit.

The doctor received the blessing of the Lord and through the anointing, decided to build his health center. He was praying to have the energy to go forward and develop the best natural vitamins for his clients. He wanted the Lord to help him give them the best opportunity for full and complete wellness.

TRANSLATION: EPHESIANS (NIV) 1:18

The hope we have is not a vague feeling that the future will be positive, but it is complete assurance of certain victory through God. This complete certainly comes to us through the Holy Spirit who is working in us.

Chapter Three

TRUST, HAVE PATIENCE GOD WONDERS NEVER CEASE II

Psalm 118:24 (KJV) This is the day which the Lord hath made; we will rejoice and be glad in it.

On Thursday night after the Tuesday's doctor visit, I was not feeling well. On Friday, I called the doctor and explained to him about my nervous stomach and rest room movements. He said, from what he was hearing, all is going well. He offered to pencil me into an open 5:00 p.m. if I wanted to come in.

I told the doctor on the phone, there were some spiritual attachments to why I felt uneven. I told him, I received a message in my spirit that there's a previous concern that had not been noted earlier in the day.

I needed to see the doctor to get an up-to-date analysis on my health status even though he felt certain, on the phone, that things were well. At his office, he began his examination and gave me my first good news.

The nervousness in my stomach had to do with my stomach moving into realignment. My stomach was previously out of alignment before doctor made adjustments. Now the organs were slowly turning into right position.

My immune system had increased from 600 points on Tuesday to 1000 on Friday. My previous level of 600 was very low which indicated that it must be raised for my strength to return.

Family, I confess, working long hours, days and months without proper rest and eating habits, will bring about burn-out.

Before the doctor completed his work, I was prompted by The Holy Spirit to bless him with authority to use the name of Jesus in his work. This would give the doctor greater authority working with his patients and established the things he desired to come to fruition.

For me, he is and excellent doctor, in his field as a naturopathic doctor. He's humble as he works on his patients through the Holy Spirits guidance.

The doctor now has greater insight to evaluate his patient's issues and prepare their prescriptions. I thank God for trusting me with such powerful words that strengthen others to do greater work in the name of Jesus. The provision of the Lord never ceases. The Lord is our Jehovah-Jireh, I thank you for increase.

TRANSLATION: SCRIPTURE; PSALMS 118:24

There are days when the last thing we want to do is rejoice. Our mood is down, our situation is out of hand and our sorrow or guilt is overwhelming. We can relate to the psalmist who often felt this way, no matter how low David felt, he trusted in the Lord. We are to always be honest with God, when we talk with Him, we end our prayers in praise. When we don't feel like rejoicing, we are to tell God how we truly feel, and He will give us a reason to rejoice. Let us take this day, He has given us and be glad in it.

Chapter Four

HE GROWS US

Psalm 92:14 (NIV) They will still bear fruit in old age, they will stay fresh and green:

As the Holy Spirit matures us, we often don't understand why we are going through so much difficulty. Chastisement are necessary for the Holy Spirit to shape us, mold us and prepare us for his next level, we admittedly don't know the mind of Christ, this began to teach us about trusting His most Holy name know matter what.

Assuredly, He has our best interest planned out for us, we will learn to trust the Lord, are stay in chastisement.

I am now at my regular natural path to follow up on

my joints, I learn from the receptionist, I was a day early, I apologize, the doctor was alright with my mistake. He began with a powerful prayer in the Lord for my joints, and before he came into the room, I had prayed and invited the Holy Ghost and the Angels to come and minister with him for me.

After my exam, my basic need was to exercise, get a good regiment of vitamins to restore the lost substance. He was about to leave the room, I was curious how he gets his understanding of our conditions other than exams.

I said in my mind, I wonder if he has spiritual insight to look at our organs, this would help him determine the necessary treatment more accurately for better results. I was considering blessing him, it wouldn't be the first time the Lord used His servant. Thank you, Lord.

I felt His beautiful presence in my spirit, the prompting of the Holy Spirit to pray and anoint him with spiritual insight. I spoke this to him, he quickly said I receive it. I said you heard the Lord say anoint you, he said yes. I anointed his mind and hands with the spiritual blessing upon his life with insight and revelation. You are now quickened to make more accurate examinations, for us who like less invasive exams.

While lying there on the table, I doze off and had a most unusual vision. I saw old fashion irons, like the ones we iron our cloths with in the old days, perhaps four of them, I believe. These irons moved swiftly over my stomach, ironing in every direction. The doctor had gone out, I was not certain what was happening. The thought that came to mind, you can cauterize wounds like this to seal or bind the wound.

While typing this, I felt the Lord presence and I am thankful for the knowledge and understanding.

During this period of meditation, I continued in the vision and I saw the area of concern and prayed for a touch from the Holy Spirit to heal me, as only He can. The Holy Spirit prompted me that I did see the area of concern and I am praying for His blessing of a healing.

For me, this was a powerful move of the Lord, growing this young man, the young doctor is obedient to the Lord, who gives him instructions in prayer. I can see and feel the shaping of this young doctor who will be doing great and wonderful works for the Lord, who is preparing him to fulfill his purpose for the Lord.

TRANSLATION: PSALMS 92:14: (NIV)

God isn't restricted to young people who seem to have unlimited strength and energy. Even in old age, devoted believers can produce spiritual fruit. There are many faithful older people who continue to have a fresh outlook and can teach us from lifetime experiences, of serving God.

Such out and elderly friend or relative to tell you about his or her experiences with the Lord, they can challenge you to new heights of spiritual growth. "His presence was felt when I read this."

Chapter Five

TRUST, HAVE PATIENCE

Isaiah 54:17: (NIV) Know weapon forged against you will prevail and you will refute every tongue that accuses you. This is the heritage of the servants of the Lord, and this is there vindication from me.

We are all on a journey, many of us are seeking the Lord for the correct way too be led by the Lord, then we will be certain to walk in our purpose that has been prepare for us from the beginning.

Many of us follow other visions and their purpose, but it was clear to me in order to be with the Father, we must come to Him through His Son.

In the morning when I rise, I'm looking to fill whole and energize in all parts of my body and when I don't feel the surging energy, I get to my prayer quarters and tell my Lord all about how I feel. I know He already knows, but He wants to hear from me and from you as well. On a particular morning my left knee felt sore and stiff, so I prayed for my knee and laid hands on it with anointing oil. I said to the Lord it's alright if He give me a touch, I like for Him to put His hands on me.

I went back to bed and slept very well, I had a vision, I saw this writing board the teachers use in classrooms to write on when they are teaching.

In the left corner of the green board, there was writing in very large letters, "WORKOUT," I woke quickly with clarity and understanding. If the Lord is telling me to workout, the body is stronger than I had supposed, so I began to exert more exercise, because He is telling me my health is more improved than I think it is.

A short while later, I realize my left knee was feeling very healthy, I laugh to myself and through my hands in the air and praise the Lord, I realize I had received my touch from Him as well. Family, I capture this moment with the Lord hearing my prayer, He look at my heart and fulfilled my prayer according to His will. Heavenly Father, I worship You as the Lord of my life; may all the praises, thanksgiving, and worship continually be before You from our household and the families that support this ministry.

A few years ago, I am remembering on a Sunday afternoon a long week had me under stress, I weren't feeling so great, I kneel down and began to pray, thanking the Lord for all He had done, is doing, and going to do. While on my knees I felt this rush and became overwhelm and were brought to tears, I had a feeling I needed prayer, I asked for my sister, my Reverend Nancy to pray for me, we were very closed, she is in heaven and I felt in my spirit to ask the Lord for her prayers. She always had words of comfort for me when life trials are on every front.

I left my bedroom lounge chair where I was in prayer and went into my closet and lay on the floor and still in tears, I couldn't understand why I was so disturbed, suddenly this arm came up under me and I was totally surprised and asked myself what this means.

When this arm rose up under my shoulder, I felt a calmness immediately wondering what just happen to me. I was in prayer, asking for my sister who is in glory with the Lord to pray for me and the righteous arm of the Lord appeared and comforted me.

The rush that came against me, was the enemy, because of the work I was doing in the streets of Atlanta with the homeless. I assured them this is why I am here, "I am sent by the Lord," to give you His assurance that you aren't forgotten. There were those that gave their life to Christ on those corners and their lives were changed.

Truth be told, if Satan began to lose those who he claimed, he gets an attitude and attacks the Lords saints. For me, the Lord's righteous arm became my covering, He promised to protect us when we are down in the valley of despair, resurrecting our sisters and brothers with the word of the Lord, that there is a better way.

Our Lord is always on time, I had gotten up from the floor and washed my face when I heard my cellphone giving me notification that I had received text messages from my therapist, a natural-path at a Wholeness Center. I looked at the time and noticed it came through while I was in prayer for help. It reads "For some reason you are on my heart today, have a blessed day".

"I put a Hedge of Protection around you and sent you healing, love, and blessings," I think of you often and you were a pivotal force in my life.

I took a trip out of town to get back on my regiment, exercises, eating, juicing and body massages at this

Wholeness Center out of town. I wanted a lymphatic therapist that was quite spiritual and thorough. I chose the therapist they suggested, she was regarded as highly qualified in this field.

Just as she began to work on me, I got this warm and fulfilling feeling from the Lord, to anoint her hands and bless them. I prayed that the Lord would bless her with sight, the revelation to see, and understand how to address greater needs in her work as a therapist. I explained to her, the Lord requires this of her before she could work on me.

Now you have authority with the Lord, I call you into His ministry of the gospel of Jesus Christ, you are fully endowed as His chosen.

On Monday, I believe I entered a two day fast, hoping through prayer and quiet time with the Lord, He would shed light on my becoming weak and filled with tears. I had begun a thank you Lord prayer and something came over me. I was in fear and tears, in my closet. I called my prayer partner, Prophetess Cathy and shared my story on what transpired.

She replied, that she received in the spirit that I had received the, "The Arm of The Lord for Protection.

These trials make us partners with Christ in His

suffering, so we can share in His glory, when it is revealed to the world.

TRANSLATION: ISAIAH 54:17

This scripture assures us, that we will get attacks in our service for the Lord, but in those negative encounters, there in is the arm of the Lord to cover us and go through the storms and situations that life is handing us. We have the Word of the Lord if we trust Him fully. Know weapon turned against you shall succeed, and you will have justice in every courtroom lie.

Chapter Six

A ROD AND STAFF

Psalm 23:4 (NIV) Even though I walk through the valley of the shadow of death, I will fear no evil, for you are with me, your rod and your staff, they comfort me.

I was in the woods cutting down trees and saw this hickory limb and selected it because we who know hickory wood will verify it is a very hard and durable wood as it seasons it becomes a comforter in unplanned situations. I try to avoid leaving my house without my walking stick, I even take it with me in my car.

The Lord called it to be my comfort from Him. A word like that allows me to be not only thankful but have His personal hand about me.

This habit of having a walking stick has dwelled within me since early childhood. Our dad always had a walking stick when he went into the woods. Growing up on the farm, you didn't want to get caught between the house and the woods without having support to help, especially if you encounter a mean dog, snake, or a kid bigger than you were.

The stick has always been the equalizer from the days of my youth until today in my late seventies, I have my walking stick. I don't remember for certain if I was calling it the pole, my Moses stick first, I do distinctly remember my grandson, Naji, calling me Moses affectionally after seeing the television version of Moses with a gray beard, he deemed me Moses.

Most of the time you will find me outside, around my house or someone else's home, you'll find me with a firm stick and keep it with me. I am remembering the second trip to West Africa, Monrovia, Liberia, we were on a tour day into the woods, immediately as we walked along the narrow trails, I located me a walking stick.

Our Pastor was leading us, with the tour guide in front and I was bringing up the rear as the last person. When we arrived at the swinging bridges, the pastor pleasantly said to me, "you will need to get rid of that Moses stick", as I would need both hands to hold and balance walking across the swinging bridges, all seven of them, I accepted healthy advice and collected my walking stick on my return.

A few months after we had arrived home from our last tour stop and flight back from Accra, Ghana.

I had my comfortable walking stick with me in my car, on the road to see my older brother at a care facility, this conviction came over me while driving. I was listening to a CD, the minister was preaching and when she spoke on the uses of Moses walking stick with revelation, knowledge, and under the anointing. I realized it had to be anointed, Reverend Alphonso, my younger brother, came into my spirit. I told him about my encounter and how the Lord moved upon me to get it anointed, he said "I'll be right there".

Reverend Alphonso came with his anointing oil, on his arrival he took the beautiful hickory stick and began bathing it in the anointing oil.

After a few minutes, he said "hey bro, feel this", I ran my hands up and down it the way he was doing but I didn't feel anything.

A few minutes later he shook his hand and said feel it now, the hickory stick was hot to my hands, we stood there praising the Lord and wondered how we would use it to give the Lord His glory.

The Lord would be upon it and it's uses, I adopted my Moses walking stick, through the guidance of the Holy Spirit, it became my anointed Rod and Staff. The Holy Spirit took it further and deemed it a Rod of Power and a Staff of Grace and Peace that I can only receive through Him. I am convicted by His presence and I gave thanks and all the glory to the Lord.

TRANSLATION: PSALMS 23:4 (NIV)

The work of righteousness in peace. In these paths we cannot walk, unless, God lead us into them, and lead simply trust our Shepherds care, and hearken to his voice. The valley of the shadow of death may denote the most severe and terrible affliction, or dark dispensation of providence, that the psalmist ever could come under. Between the part of the flock on earth and that which is in heaven,

Death lies like a dark valley that must be passed in going from one to the other. But even in this there are words which lessen the terror. It is but the shadow of death: the shadow of a serpent will not sting, nor the shadow of a sword kills.

Chapter Seven

THUS, SAYS THE LORD

Proverb 16:3: (NIV) Commit to the Lord, whatever you do, and your plans will succeed.

Some of us make commitments in the name of the Lord, to get a task, or personal matters given to the Lord to come into fruition. Often, given this task to the Lord is a superficial act, when we are really calling the task for ourselves and getting the credit. When circumstances become difficult, we remember it is the Lord who can do all things, and we give it over to Him, temporarily.

There is a delicate balance of giving the task to the Lord for it to succeed. This doesn't mean we are to settle back and fail to be diligent in applying ourselves but trusting the work of the Lord to guide you and know that aside from "the Lord we can do nothing."

If I am looking at a major task or health circumstances and I believe that I am depending on the Lord to guide us through this tremendous financial and health circumstances. If I haven't done this correctly, I will establish it now.

I welcome the Holy Spirit of God, to guide not only myself, but the family because we all are affected. Our young friend has this tour company, my wife and I have supported our friend in this endeavor.

I believe that I have prayed and trusted the Lord to bring to fruition the plan effort to pay for the equipment and purchases of land that will give him the facility to set the business into full service.

He will have the space, great location and can share with others who also may need parking and staging vehicles spaces.

I drive by the location and see the building there in my spirit through the Lord, praying only to Him for this effort to materialize. When this land was first spoken about, I confessed to the Lord, we had funds, I was depending on Him to help this to come through, if it's His will. I left the papers at the bank to process for the loan, the Holy Spirit told me to anoint the documents and I did.

My health situation is in His hands, I listen for His instruction and I pray. When I hear, I want to obey the Holy Spirit only. I need health and strength to become the prophet you are training me to be.

By myself, I can't restore my health, but through the Lord, I pray right now, that His will is to continue to strengthen me into good health.

I can do mission work abroad into West Africa, where I have met several majors, and chieftains there, I would like to do mission work, to the Lord be the glory.

While completing the courses towards my Master of Theology, the Holy Spirit help me to know, He is my teacher and I love and accept this.

My health has been questionable at times, I have asked the Lord to allow me to complete assignments that he have been set before me. I have always prayed for longevity and have tried to live a healthy life style. I requested that The Lord bless me with fifteen years to continue His work for completion. I thought I felt unction from the Holy Spirit that said yes.

TRANSLATION: PROVERB 16:3; (NIV)

There are several ways we commit our works to the Lord and take responsibility back when the plan of the Lord isn't going the way we expect them. Our task sometimes goes fully to the Lord and we remove ourselves completely from it, and believe we are trusting the Lord for its tremendous success. If we take ourselves out of God's hands, He can't work through us to develop us and grow your plan.

There is a delicate balance to accomplish our work by giving it to the Lord and trusting Him to bring it to completion but realize we are part of the working for the success of our assignments.

PART II
HIS WORD

All scriptures are given by inspiration of God, and is profitable for doctrine, for reproof, for correction, for instruction in righteousness.

There is a real need in the body of Christ today for stability. This stability comes from only one source, God's Word. With so many winds of doctrine flying around today it can be very difficult to discern that which is truth, from that which is error. It is my hope and prayer that our ministry can help you locate God's truth; for the truth can and will set you free. May the Lord keep you in these times as you are pressing in for a deeper relationship with Him.

Chapter One

MESSAGES IN OUR DREAMS I

Psalm 90:17 (NIV) May the favor of the Lord our God rest on us; establish the work of our hands for us-yes, establish the work of our hands.

Earlier this week a friend gave me a message the Holy Spirit had given her in a dream or vision. When my friend first heard the words from the dream it led her to believe it was for her. The dream continued, as she listens and realize it wasn't for her, but me.

My working outside with my workers suggested I am applying my energy in the wrong places. The Lord wants me to apply my best efforts to the work He has assigned me. At this age, laboring on my lawn, cutting down trees and painting isn't the assignment, I should be trying to fulfill. The Lord has reminded me in the pass, get back on your assignments where I have sent you for the Father will be glorified.

"Oscar, let the people follow the schedule and do their work", this is in reference to the workers along with my brother to handle the work outside and trust them to manage it. I'm to focus on my assignments. I'm remembering, I had been outside giving instructions and corrections, perhaps too much; this takes away from my writing, visitation at the nursing homes and my theology studies.

Perhaps a week later, in the morning, in my vision, I heard a familiar voice say, "There was something I was supposed to tell you." I said, "that sounds like my close friend," I could see a glimpse of her in my vision. I seemed to have already been humming a song I had heard from a gospel artist. The song says, "The Lord wants all of you, all of your love." I believe her song is a message from the Lord, calling her to a closer relationship to Him, so He can grow her into her purpose that He had prepared for her from the beginning. In many cases, we are working in our assignments, but we haven't submitted our will to the Lord, to serve Him only.

A song began to come into my spirit, "I Surrender All," as I started singing a few lines, it bothered me and gave me a feeling of uneasiness that I haven't gotten back on course.

This tells me I must pay close attention and stay on my assignment's, I'm not certain what is in the rest of the vision. Better yet I am going to see what the "Word," is saying, so I won't be making excuses why I didn't get it right. "I Surrender All," Romans 6:13; Don't continue offering or yielding your bodily members (and faculties) to sin as instruments of (tools) of wickedness. But offer and yield yourselves to God as though you have been raised from the dead to (perpetual) life, and your bodily members (and faculties) to God, presenting them as implements of righteousness. Oh! How the Lord leads us, we may not understand where He is taking us, even though our fear has a grip on us, we will trust the Lord and be obedient.

These last two visions were in relationship and I wanted to understand the deeper meaning in order to be in right alignment to follow the direction the Holy Spirit is taking me. The scripture made clear, don't waiver between two opinions, there is only one who has our best in His heart, and if we trust Him, He will bring it into fruition.

The understanding I am getting now, I believe the Lord has a time table for me to complete my writings. Perhaps something is coming with a fixed time and perhaps the Lord wants me to be prepared for it. When I wrote this, I felt His presence very strongly.

There is joy in the Lord, when he gives us understanding, when He give us information in our dreams and sends a witness.

My brother calls and said he was on the way to my home, he was thinking about our friend and how strong she is in-spite of what she has been going through with the loss of her dear friend. The Lord is leading me to bring understanding to her for the ministry, He has plans for her life. The Lord had His eyes upon her for a while and it is her time now to serve the Lord. He is the only one can say, "I will never leave you nor forsake you".

TRANSLATION: PSALMS 90:17 (NIV)

Because our days are numbered, we want our work to count, to be effective and productive. We desire to see God's eternal revealed now and for our work to reflect his permanence. If we feel dissatisfied with this life and all its imperfections, remember our desire to see our work in placed there by God, that desire can only be satisfied in eternity.

Chapter Two

MESSAGES IN OUR DREAMS II

I Peter 3:15: (KJV) But Sanctify the Lord God in your hearts: and be ready always to give an answer to every man that asketh you a reason of the hope that is in you with meekness and fear.

The Lord has our purpose all planned for us from the beginning. This is one of the single greatest acts of our Lord, getting us in right alignment so we can grow and be prosperous in Him. "The Message in our Dreams," speaks to how the Lord continues to work with us to receive His assignments and proclaim His works.

I made several attempts to reach my friend who lives out of town because she was in my dream and spoke a word that left me concerned. She commented, "I intended to tell you something," I recognized her voice and wondered what that could be. We hadn't talked since I visited her several months ago. I was concentrating on our last visit, what important conversation did we have, and what I neglected to follow up on. During those moments I dozed off to sleep and I heard this song, that was very popular and rewarding doing those times.

It was inspirational, it spoke to your spirit and left a question to be answered, have I given my all to my Lord? I finally connected with my friend, I informed her I had been trying to reach her. I heard your voice in my dream, and this song I like very much. I find myself often humming it and it's in my spirit by now. She tells me, she's having poor sleeping habits and wasn't answering the phone often.

Oscar, what is the name of the song, "The Lord Wants It All," that's my favorite song, I sing it all the time. You have been in my spirit and my mind, the Lord wants you to know, He has you in His arms and your unrest will rest in His arms and peace be upon you now.

In the future, you must learn to be obedient, I believe you have been hearing my name in your dreams, I felt this in my spirit. My friend admitted she has heard my name in her dreams.

In my prayers for you now, the Lord will protect you and to let you know, you have a personal covenant with Him. He wants you to know, you have a beautiful spirit, helping so many others, this is your calling, to serve others through the Lord. The Lord is asking, will you serve Him? Not your way, but His will must be done.

While we were talking, I felt a fresh anointing go out to her, I prayed the comfort of an angel be sent to her for comfort and company when she has unrest. "The Lord Wants It All," is her calling into the ministry of the Lord Jesus Christ. You have been doing the work, now accept His awesome assignments by submitting to His will to be done through you, it's a "High Calling," to serve our Lord and Savior, Jesus Christ.

TRANSLATION: I PETER: 3:15

We sanctify God before others, when our conduct invites and encourages them to glorify and honor him. What was the ground and reason of their hope? We should be able to defend our religion with meekness, in the fear of God. There is no room for any other fears where this great fear is; it disturbs not.

Chapter Three

HE SENDS A WORD

Isaiah 54:8 (NIV) I hid my face from you for a moment, but with everlasting kindness, I will have compassion on you," says the Lord your Redeemer.

Family, so often we call the name of our Lord, asking for help, rather it would give more sincerity to our prayers if we are in a situation of poor health, family issues, children and grandchildren working our very last nerve. I've learned to take a step back and question how all this mess got this far out of hand? Often, we are in prayer and continuing in prayer stressing the Lord to do this and do that.

Lord, I know you can because the word says, you have all power and can do all things, but leaving out, if it's your will, oh merciful Lord, mighty God, let it be done, "the glory is all thine Oh Most High."

In our prayer life to the Lord, our first and foremost effort is to require His presence in our life, the Lord promises to fight our battles, and defeat every enemy that comes after us. It is rewarding to hear the Lord say, He fought every battle for His King David and none of his enemies escaped. This is the Lord's vindication for us that He speaks to in Isaiah 54:17. "No weapon that is formed against thee shall prosper; and every tongue that rises against thee in judgment thou shalt condemn." This is the heritage of the servants of the Lord, and their righteousness is of me, saithe the Lord." This is our vindication from the Lord, to learn to trust Him in every event and situation that comes into our lives.

The wife and I received a message from our Reverend family member. She questions, "what's going on over there with you all"? "The Lord brought your face and name before me, and I am wondering what's going on with the family that He has me calling the Lord's name in the night watch and early in the morning. The Lord has given me and assignment, come over to the house and we can begin our work according to His word."

The Lord instructs the pastor to inform me get plenty of rest and expect improved health over this time period. Time and time again you work too many days, too many long hours.

You can't say yes to every asking, you promised to be a better manager of your work and protect your health in your latter years. You will enjoy more time with your wife of over 55 years, plus the joy of seeing and spending time with your great-grandchildren.

On one occasion in particular, my son came into my office and asked me to just say yes, he had a surprise for me. I knew there was a catch, but I still said, "yes." He said, "good deal pops, we are leaving early Friday morning for the beach in Florida to celebrate your birthday". "You will have all the fun you can handle this weekend with your grand and great-grandchildren. Uninterrupted fun on the beaches in the sand." My son, Oscar Lee has a sweet spirit about him, there are things he does for others that he never talks about. He reminds me in some ways of his grand-pa, Reverend Frank with the helpful countenance. He says, "by the way, thanks for saying yes, it made getting you out of town and away from your workload easier."

I prayed to the Lord, asking Him for strength that will

help me through another overload of work on my desk and the ministry. Family I thought I was managing well, and before I realized it, I was overloaded.

It seems the Lord was working it out all ready, our reverend family member had been summoned by the Lord to gather us in prayer.

Afterwards we began communion for 40 days, and I find myself in bed early and let the energy return, primarily from resting.

Thank you, Lord, the message here, if we are trusting the Lord, plan to do his assignment, and learn patience we won't find ourselves overly tired with our knees knocking for a lack of rest. Allowing time for recovery, saying prayers, reading scriptures, and believing in the Lord will guide us in the days to come and I am thankful and blessed the "Lord Sends A Word."

TRANSLATION: ISAIAH 54:8

The God we serve is holy, and He cannot tolerate sin. When his people blatantly sinned, God in His anger chose to punish them. Sin separates us from God and brings us pain and suffering. But if we confess our sin and repent, then God will forgive us. Have you ever been separated from a loved one and the experienced joy when that person returned? That is like the joy God experiences when you repent and return to Him.

Chapter Four

ALWAYS PRAY

Psalm 33:8: I will instruct you and teach you in the way you should go: I will counsel you and watch over you.

When we say yes to the Lord, we are on our journey for a life time, if we are patient in our learning and realize we are led by the Holy Spirit and stay the course we will get there. We will have many distrusting times, that will take us into valleys of despair, every time one storm ends another one is waiting around the bend.

I try to figure out what I did wrong, who did I mistreat Lord, and how did I drop the ball that is causing all this confusion in my life? I am frightened and in a state of fear, I feel like I can't get out of my mess, I need you Lord.

What prayer can I pray, hopefully the Lord will hear me? Earlier years in my prayer life, seeking the Lord, trying to become a worthy servant, hoping the Lord would reveal His need for me. Traveling alone this difficult process seeking the Lord and hoping to grow during these times. There was this occasion, I had an issue with a dear friend and it turned into an argument. I said more than I should have and later when I cooled off, I became disturbed, even frightened that the Lord was going to chastise me. My rudeness and being disrespectful to my dear friend, my action wasn't becoming that of a child of the most "High God."

I was scared and begging forgiveness with every breath. I knew the Lord was going to nail my hide to the barn door. "To nail your hide to the barn," refers to the father in the old days who would beat his son for disobedience and left him mentally bruised and physically scarred for life.

Every day at two or three in the morning, I was praying to the Lord, forgive me for I had sin against Him first and then my friend. I realize it was an ordinary matter, I should have overlooked the issue and approached it in a more civilized way.

I was terribly worried by my action, this was very early in my ministry and I didn't know just how severe my chastisement from the Lord would turn out. Finally, one morning I was down on the floor lamenting before the Lord of all, He said to me; "Oscar, I heard you the first time, pray forgiveness and keep my assignments present in your spirit", I looked around to see if the Lord was fully present in my prayer quarters with me.

I am remembering when I first began visiting care facilities, park benches and having prayer with those I encountered along the way. I believe these are those the Lord set in our pathways, desiring for them to know more about Him. There are men and women I have met that are looking to come to the Lord. They are backsliders desiring to return to Him. I have prayed with many who have come through challenges only by the grace of the Lord, they affirmed, turning their lives over to the Lord and trusting in Him.

The Holy Spirit blessed me with a prayer warrior, who grew in their walk with the Lord. We began to see a face or a name, we learn through the Lord to pray with boldness, fervently and effectual prayer to gain victory for those who come in our dreams and vision the Lord gives us.

A friend had prayed with me several times and has prayed for me many times since the Lord has given her messages and scriptures that helps me to come through my storms and gave me hope. In Luke 1:74; The Lord would grant unto us, that we, being delivered out of the hand of our enemies, might serve Him without fear. This transpired in February 2011 and I was strengthened by the word of the Lord, I am continuing to do my mission work while I work out my valley experiences in my life.

I felt the presence of the Holy Spirit, when this happened, I began to pray for her and ask His blessing upon her life, according to His will. She replied, she heard in her spirit, the Lord said, "He is careful to watch over His word and keep His promise". The Lord said: He will remove all the illness and discomforts that have bothered me.

Remember none of these events from the past, He will remove them from the root, close the gate, and they will never bother me again.

This dear sister was praying to me in the spirit and the Holy Ghost was heavy upon me and I was in tears for remembering me in the times of my valley experiences. In storms that sometimes seem endless God promises to never leave us nor forsake us, He will be with us always until the end.

TRANSLATION: Psalms 33:8

God describes some people as being like horses or mules that have to be controlled by bits and bridles. Rather than letting God guide them step by step, they stubbornly leave God only one option. If God longs to guide us with love and wisdom rather than punishment.

Chapter Five

RESTORATION

Galatians 6:10; (KJV) As we have therefore opportunity, let us do well unto all men, especially unto them who are of the household of faith.

Friday morning, I raised up early for prayer and meditation, during my struggle to meditate, I see a bowl of cereal with a spoon in it. I was alert and my mind kept wandering into negative events that had transpired, earlier in the night, each time I bring myself back to a sense of normalcy, I drift again.

I left my prayer quarters and went back to bed. Still very early in the morning I was restless, so I got back up, went into my prayer room. I applied the blood of Jesus prayer over me, the family, and everything else that may involve me in any way, I covered it in the blood of Jesus the Christ, who went to the cross for us, with His redeeming sacrifice.

I ask the Lord Jesus Christ, to wash and cleanse my mind with His Precious Blood. Give each of us clarity of thought; give us a sound and sober mind in Jesus Christ Holy name according to John 14:14; "You may ask anything in my name and I will do it." I went back to bed and the phone rang; it was a friend who was having a challenging time also. They requested prayer and I went before the Lord on their behalf, fully believing the Holy Spirit would restore them and strengthen their memory and come their fears.

Our Holy Spirit is known to go before those who trust and are willing to be led by the Holy Spirit. The Holy Spirit abounds quickly through my friend on the phone and gave her a word for me as well. The Holy Spirit began by saying, "there is something I want you to do for Me".

"My situation had been resolved", she spoke and said, "I can go back to bed, you have been restored everything will be all right, you can go to the funeral you will be fine". I went to bed and immediately the Holy Spirit whispered clearly to me, "I want you to prepare me a perfect meal," I said that I am not perfect, so I can't prepare you a perfect meal because I am not perfect, if you tell me what to do, I can do it". In the next moment I was rinsing 2 silver spoon and forks, this is a habit of mine, but I didn't see myself use them, I believe my rinsing the silverware, was to let me know this message is for me. Then I see this large cave like location and it was deep and dark looking in the distance.

I kept peering, trying to see clearly what it was, but was unsuccessful, my thoughts left me thinking what I was seeing was a small casket fit for a baby with a white lining in it. I was troubled by my dream or vision and left wondering, what's going on with me and I remember the Holy Spirit said I was restored; everything would be all right.

It is about 11:00 am Saturday morning, I saw my youngest brother with my workers outside painting, I decided to go out and talk with him about my dreams and visions. He is a minister well learned in scriptures and theology. I asked him about the perfect meal to which he replied, here on earth we aren't perfect, but it represents maturing and growth, and in this instance, it would be maturing in Christ Jesus.

The next thing I asked him about was the two silver spoons and two silver forks, that I was rinsing off, but I didn't see myself use them.

Reverend Alphonso commented that silver represent authority and perhaps it's telling me to avoid areas that have me making repetitive actions toward issues or situations. He said, learn to make precise decisions, walk away and leave it to the Lord to render what is good and perfect in His sight.

There are many individuals who don't want any change in their life and lifestyles but are always approaching and asking for spiritual guidance. Even in these circumstances to those who don't know the Lord, we offer to leave a word from the Lord, that no one can see the Father unless they submit to the Son, learn of Him, and accept Him as their Savior. Many of us have walked on the wild side of life, a time comes to all of us, when we will need a Savior. Next, I told my brother of the cave where I saw something that looked like a small casket with a white lining in it and the minister said, some time a setting like that can be abstract and doesn't mean anything in particular.

These explanations were somewhat settling, but I feel uneasy and will continue seek the answers, so I can get in right alignment and follow instruction.

The sister on the phone called for prayer and gave me and instruction from the Lord. The Lord said to her, "I want Oscar to do something for Me." I want him to reserve special time for me.

Today at my doctor's appointment, I get my second request from the Lord. My Natural-Path doctor always prays for me, before he begins his work. He began having prayer for me, and in his prayer, he said the Lord wanted me to choose some specific time for Him and follow it for 14 days. I was a little surprised, getting a powerful word like this back to back. I realized I had to get aboard and began my fast. This would be a sacrifice or fast that I would do for Him. This is part of planning to spend time with Him through prayer, meditation and being in His presence.

This could very well be that meal for two, with the silver forks and spoon that had appeared. I remembered this, even if the interpretation of the vision or dreams were not completely correct, planning to spend special time with the Lord is challenging, to say the least.

To me it's a wilderness experience, being in the presence of the "Most High God," and through my scriptures, my prayers, fasting, and waiting to hear from the Lord. On an occasion He said to me, "Oscar, I have chosen you, I know longer call you servant, but my friend." The power of His voice left me shaken and helpless, and even weak in the knees.

Going forward, I fast every week of every month at least two days a week or more to learn about the Lord and how best to serve Him. Our level of communication improved, I believe I was developing a personal relationship with the Lord.

These events in my journals are so personal, but I share them with the family because I hope this will help others to take time and build your own personal relationship with the Lord. Perhaps you will call His name in a moment of great need and you will see Him in the spirit, lean forward and lend you His ear to let you know, He hears your prayers and will answer them according to His will.

TRANSLATION: GALATIANS 6:10; (KJV)

There is divine blessing that the Lord bring upon us when we do good; believers are urged to seize each opportunity to do good. Doing good refers to the ministry of restoration with the leading of the Holy Spirit and perseverance generally. Believers are to minister first unto them who are Christian of the faith and unto the rest of the world.

Chapter Six

FOR A MOMENT; HE HID HIS ANGER

Mark 6:34(KJV)And Jesus, when he came out, saw much people, and was move with compassion towards them, because they were as sheep not having a shepherd: and he began to teach them many things

I received this scripture very early after mid-night, I had just retired for bed about 12:15 a.m., immediately I began to dream and have this vision; I saw myself playing softball, the setting was in my younger days in an old field not far from our home.

I hit the ball and ran for first base and it was a long drive, I turn first base and headed for second base and from behind, someone tackles me around my shoulders from my left side, and with only a glance, it looked like a family member's son.

I continued and end up on second base, I tackle the person to the ground and put my forearm under there neck and said in an angry voice, "you don't know who I am, what I have done," when I look in the person face, I had only a glance and it look like a dear friend, I know the father. He seemed to have a smile on his face, he said "Mark, chapter 6 is all right for you." I receive this from our prophetic minister, giving prophesy into, perhaps my future, it seems as if I am always on a journey for the Lord. I received Mark chapter 6.

I read 56 verses and decide to write one verse for this chapter, it is in relationship to mission work for our Jesus Christ and his disciples are to seek those who are lost and healing the sick and afflicted.

Christ despised in his own country:

Mark 6:1-2 (NIV) Jesus left there and went to his hometown, accompanied by his disciples. (2) When the Sabbath came, he began to teach in the synagogue, and many who heard him were amazed. "Where did this man get these things?" they asked.

"What's this wisdom that has been given him? What are these remarkable miracles he is performing?

Translation: *Christ despised in his own country; Our Lord's countrymen tried to prejudice the minds of people against him. Is not this the carpenter? Our Lord Jesus probably had worked in that business with his father. How much did these Nazarenes lose by obstinate prejudices against Jesus! May Divine grace deliver us from that unbelief.*

The next morning, I read the chapter and was looking for the meaning. Earlier that afternoon I had received a text scripture from my nephew, I read it several times for understanding. I am working on a sermon for my homiletically class, doing my study, I read this scripture and felt the prompting by the Holy Spirit. I included the scripture in my material and later I began to wonder if this were meant for me beyond my classroom preparation and delivery of sermons.

I visited my commentaries for support, hopeful to receive information and get understanding and see where I took the wrong path, if I don't find my wrongs, it is difficult by any measure to correct and be able to seek the Lord for forgiveness. We must have truth and revelation to have a relationship with the Lord Jesus Christ, He is the only one I know, who loves me in-spite of me.

The Glory of Zion:

Isaiah 54:8; (NIV)) in a surge of anger, I hid My face from you for a moment, but with everlasting kindness, I will have compassion on you, "says the Lord your Redeemer."

Translation: *It's certain deliverance: The wrath is title, the mercies great; the wrath for a moment, the kindness everlasting. The mountains have been shaken and removed, but the promises of God never were broken by any event.*

Tuesday morning, I received another scripture from him my nephew.

Judges 5:11; "They that are delivered from the noise of archers in the places of drawing water, they shall rehearse the righteous acts toward the inhabitants of his villages in Israel: then shall the people of the Lord go down to the gates."

Translation: *The distress and deliverance of Israel:*

At all times Satan will endeavor to hinder the believer from drawing near to the throne of grace. Notice God's kindness to his trembling people. It is the glory of God to protect those who are most exposed, and to help the weakest.

The gates refer to a scene of legal and business activity in many instances, in Ruth chapter 4:1 it refers to Boaz met his relative there to discuss business, there were the city elders called to witness this transaction and to hold it legal for Boaz and his kinsman. I received early in the morning.

I am receiving scriptures, I am studying them through my commentaries to get the intended prophesy for myself and the ministry. I am affected by the meaning and I need to correct those unrighteous acts that I have made and pray forgiveness from the Lord and repent of my mistakes and sins against God.

Boaz marries Ruth: Ruth 4:1; Meanwhile Boaz went up to the town gate and sat down there just as guardian-redeemer he had mentioned came along. Boaz said, "Come over here, my friends and sit down." So, he went and sat down.

Translation: Kinsman refuses to redeem Ruth's inheritance. This matter depended on the laws given by Moses about inheritance, and doubtless the whole was settled in the regular and legal manner. This kinsman, when he heard the conditions of the bargain, refused it.

TRANSLATION: (KJV) MARK 6:34

The people sought the spiritual food of Christ's word, and then he took care that they should not want bodily food. If Christ and disciples put up with mean things, surely, we may. And this miracle shows that Christ came into the world, not only to restore, but to preserve and nourish spiritual life; in him there is enough for all that come.

Chapter Seven

Exodus 14:16; (KJV) Raise your staff and stretch out your hand over the sea to divide the water so that the Israelites can go through the sea on dry ground.

I believe that the Holy Spirit placed this dream or vision in the heart of my son and it has not left him. I recall my son saying, he can't tell me where this dream or vision of a transportation company came from. I approve of him keeping it within himself who planted this enormous seed in his heart and promised him if he trusted the Lord, he would grow him and the dream.

From the time Oscar Lee engaged in gathering documentation and getting the required documents to work in this state I was drawn into this work because it was difficult trying to meet the requirements due to continuous incomplete information given to us from various departments. This theme continued into purchasing of his coaches. Whatever information that was given there was always a call for one more piece. I found myself continually in prayer before the Holy Spirit on behalf of the ASLS, A GOGO COMPANY. We were at a network meeting, and the department head, asked Oscar Lee what GOGO stood for, he stated, "God Owned, God Operated" the lady and the department head were both shocked and surprised but didn't comment. Most assuredly the Lord touched the hearts and minds of those in the banks, because the purchases were approved.

Oscar Lee taught me some things about many issues that developed and who was doing what to him, among business associates. He wouldn't hold conversation or engage in negative output from anyone. I thoroughly appreciated this growth and maturity in establishing his leadership abilities. I always believe if the Holy Spirit chose to grow you and you are obedient to that call, surely the Lord is with you. The Holy Spirit says Oscar Senior, I will guide and bless their needs and you stay focus on the ministry that I call you to. I tried some personal coaching with Oscar Lee, some off it may have been good and some the Holy Spirit was very clear, I was out of place. I perhaps realized immediately that I said or did somethings wrong and apologize to my son and like the gentleman he is, he was forgiving of me, but the Holy Ghost accepts our repentance, but He chasten those He love.

I confess, the Holy Spirit has always dealt with me bountifully, it is my prayer that He is merciful and that I am able to continue in the ministry He is teaching me in.

A few weeks ago, Oscar Lee was driving near home and saw a sign with land for sale, he made the call to see if it was available, he went to his bank and told them of his desire to purchase the land and that he wanted them to partner with him. The bank seemed very hospitable and willing, but once we applied, they provided us with contention. Through prayer and guidance, the Holy Spirit directed us to the right places and we were blessed.

The Holy Spirit called Gloria and I to forty days of Communion with Him and within those forty days, He called me to fourteen days of personal fast and prayer with Him.

This is scary to me, but never the less, I greet the Lord with enthusiasm and hoping to hear and understand Him in those quiet times of prayer and meditation. During these days, the Lord has grace on me through the extension of His love and tender mercies in my hours of need. He truly blessed my health in ways I can't explain, and I can sincerely say I am thankful, He has all my praise, honor and the glory are all His.

Early this Sunday morning after prayer, I was in meditation and I heard this strong voice say, "Wait, for A Word from the Lord," I woke before I could get His word, I believe I would hear later. While in The Community Church service, the pastor preached from Exodus, fourteenth chapter, but when he preached on verse sixteen, I felt the Holy Spirit so strongly, I began to cry and wanted to shout when the pastor said raise your staff and the power of God perform this miracle and the sea open and Israelites went across. A few minutes later, I was making a note on what I would raise my staff for and when I wrote the land for Oscar Lee, the Holy Spirit came upon me and I had received my word from the Holy Spirit from early this morning.

I called my son and he met me at the property and I took the staff and walked upon it and had Oscar Lee, Oscar Naji, and myself hold the staff and took possession of the property by asking the Lord to bless His word and the glory is His for the blessing, we are thankful. This move of the Lord was to void working through the bank, as it would not be beneficial for us.

TRANSLATION: EXODUS 14:16

The Lord told Moses stop praying and get moving. Prayer must have a vital place in our lives, but there is also place for action. Sometimes we know what to do, but we pray for more guidance as an excuse to postpone doing it.

God not only told Moses to get moving, but protect him from the Egyptian and told Moses to raise his Staff and stretch out his hand over the sea and God would bless his efforts by parting the waters, and the people could cross over on dry ground and the Lord will have His glory when The Staff is Raise again on the other side and Moses closed the Red Sea upon the Egyptian.

Chapter Eight

STAND IN THE KITCHEN

MATTHEW 9:37 (NIV) Then he said to his disciples, the harvest is plentiful, but the workers are few.

Early on Thursday morning, while meditating, I hear in my spirit, "Put in Place What I Told You to Do." I am working to put my writings in place, and with the urgent spoken Word of the Lord, along with some excellent help I am now in position to prepare for the next step.

Early this morning I heard the voice of the Lord very clearly, He said get up and "Stand in The Kitchen." I knew His voice, so I raised up and came and stood in the kitchen.

I felt His presence, so I obeyed, stood in the kitchen, and leaned on the center aisle counter. Normally, I would go into my prayer room, but I heard stand. With His breath upon me I stood and began to pray. I made certain to obey and not add disobedience to the Lord's command.

Family, you can't imagine the fear that had gripped me. I was called out of bed, commanded to stand in the kitchen and I didn't know why. The kitchen was completely dark and cold, I wish I had warmer clothes on. My right hand began to itch like crazy, then chills went down to my feet. I wondered if there was some healing going on; I heard in my spirit He was going to repair my health, some time ago.

I was praying the best I knew how, asking the Lord for understanding, forgive me for all my sins, and to help me understand my situation.

I began to try and fight through my fears, I looked up and this fist was raising up beside me at the corner of the counter that I was leaning on. I was amazed and wondered if this was the righteous and powerful hand of the Lord. I also wondered was it against me for some disobedience toward the Lord or my fellow man.

While trying to recover from this fist that rose up in front of me, I was very cold, I looked into the laundry room, I saw a pullover jersey and put it on. It was very dark when I went into the kitchen, day was breaking now. I felt weak, I took a couple of kitchen drying towels and wrapped them around my neck as a scarf, and I put pot handle pads under my elbows, the kitchen counter hadn't yielded any comfort.

I was trying to fathom what is the message for me, what great sins had I committed unto my Lord. I was in tears, I was shaking like a dried leaf. I saw feet walk down my hallway into my kitchen, I look to see where they had gone.

I looked up and behold there was my Jesus Christ hanging on the cross, amidst jagged rocks all around Him and light that shined on Him. The cross with Christ appeared in my laundry room across from the kitchen, in front of my east window where daylight was breaking through from the east.

It felt like an eternity had passed, while leaning on the kitchen counter. Wondering about the great wrongs I might have committed against the Lord and my fellow man. I wondered if it was possible, perhaps He just wanted to reveal Himself to His Oscar.

When I wrote this last statement, I felt His warm presence, and the tears did flow, what an amazing sight to behold, the Lamb of God appeared in our home. This was in

2011, September, I remember we have had other encounters, but none of the other events can rival what had just happened.

TRANSLATION: (NIV) MATTHEW 9:37

Jesus looked at the crowds following him and referred to them as a field ripe for harvest. Many people are ready to give their lives to Christ if someone would show them how. Jesus commands us to pray that people will respond to his need for workers. Often, when we pray for something, God answers our prayers by using us. Be prepared for God to use you to show another person the way to Him.

Chapter Nine

GOD MAKES PROPHETS

Romans 8:17; (KJV) And if children, then heirs of God, and joint heirs with Christ if so be that we suffer with him, that we may be also glorified together.

"His Word," is the scripture that I received over a few days continually for your servant.

August 08, 2011; I heard in my spirit, "I am going to heal you so, worship Him." When I woke up, I was humming those words, and it continued to be in my spirit. A few days later, I woke up humming a different song. I hear praise Him, over and over again.

I feel so much better since He promised to visit my health. Praise Him, over and over I sang praise him. I was quite joyful in praising the Lord, I hear "There is no body like you Lord, there is nobody like you Lord". Hear the Lord is telling and teaching me that He loves his praise, He deserves it, for He does things no one else can do.

August 23, 2011, Matthew 28:18; Everything the Father has given me, I have given you.

Learn how to walk in your spiritual body, God makes prophets, the school of Prophets train them. Apostle Bernard Jordan spoke of sight beyond sight. I felt the presence of the Holy Spirit when I heard that statement.

August 24, 2011; Isaiah 54:8, "In a surge of my anger, I hid my face from you for a moment but with everlasting, kindness I will have compassion on you, says the Lord."

I have fallen and lost communication with the Lord, I can't say how many times, but when it happens, you will know the Lord is not speaking, and the answers you seek won't come.

Job 22:28; "We can decree a thing, it shall be established. We are Kings, we must rule in the authority the Lord has given us. "Whom God Calls, He qualifies."

Proverb 16:3; "commit to the Lord whatever you do, and your plans will succeed."

Psalms 118:17; "I shall not die, but live and declare the works of God."

When I was in a Health Clinic out of town, in July 2010, I had gotten much rest, had time to fast, and learn to be patient. One morning I hear this voice in my spirit, "God isn't through with you yet," that was the encouragement I needed, thank you Lord.

TRANSLATION: (KJV) ROMANS 8:17

Many speak peace to themselves, to whom God does not speak peace. But those who are sanctified, have God's spirit witnessing with their spirit, in and by his speak peace to the soul. Though we may now seem tone losers for Christ, we shall now, we cannot, be losers by him in the end.

PART III
PRAISE

Honor rendered for worth; approval; laudation; joyful tribute or homage rendered to the Lord. The Bible makes it clear that Christians are to render to the Lord proper praise and honor, with gladness and thanksgiving for His manifold mercies and goodness to mankind.

Psalms 9:1) I will praise thee, O Lord, with my whole heart; I will show forth all thy marvellous works.

Vs. 9:11) Sing praises to the Lord, which dwelleth in Zion: declare among the people

His doings.

Chapter One

HE IS PREPARING US

Psalm 118:24 (NIV)This is the day which the Lord has made; we will rejoice and be glad in it.

I have spoken of my doctor, on numerous occasions, he is a natural pathed doctor and work powerfully through the Lord for his clients. He intercedes through the Holy Spirit for his clients, in whereas, he prays and ask of the Holy Spirit to guide his mind and with inspiration to have the capacity to work with understanding for improved health condition for his clients. Our doctor employs much efforts for our well-being, for each of us it's personal, the doctor has our improved health is his aim and fulfillment.

Before, I fully understood that the doctor prayed for us, I would always pray prior to my visit and ask of the Holy Spirit to bless the doctor and his efforts to resolve my issues concerning my health.

On this Saturday morning, the doctor invited two associates, to assist him in my total body examination by working with him on my weak areas in my body and restore it by balancing. Before the assistants can work on me, through the Holy Spirit, I bless their hands, so they could assist the doctor with balancing and restoration.

When they had finish treating me, the doctor explained that one of the sisters are considering doing communion and wanted me to speak to this. First and foremost, the Lord call me to communion and set the method. I had just finished 40 days and after two weeks I started another seven days. I explained the approach I used with my wife and myself, where as we had communion twice a day for forty days. Within the forty days, I did a fast of 14 days seeking the Lord's help in my health, my ministry, and other family issues, that seemed to come at me in several ways.

I decided to stay before the Lord to be guided and taught through these very serious issues. I believe fully the communion time I spent with the Holy Spirit made the different for me. There was a bottom line that came true for me, my immune system was charged, and I felt tremendously whole.

During the time I was still on the table I began to explain to the doctor assistants the steps we used in our communion. I felt the Holy Spirit come upon me, His presence was so fulfilling and strong I could feel the vibration as I was finishing up, I felt the Holy Spirit release me, leaving me feeling I have poured out all that I received of the Lord. The doctor spoke and said there is not a dry eye in the house, it was then I raised up and look to my left then right and saw the over-flowing of tears.

I was told there was a release from me and the spiritual release hit each of them profoundly and drew them to tears.

I was the instrument, but this was the working of the Lord in His holiness for those who desire to know more about Him, our creator. Preparing the doctor and the young assistants, the Lord want us to know they will do wonderfully well in this ministry. This ministry takes on a Lord affect for healing through faith and the Lord will direct our pass on what else is need, for myself as well.

TRANSLATION: PSALMS 118:24 (NIV)

There are days when the last thing we want to do is rejoice. Our mood is down, our situation is out of hand, and our sorrow or guilt is overwhelming. We can relate to the Psalmist, he to felt tater and torn with his burdens, but he didn't stop praising God. If we tell the Lord all about our burdens, He will give us reason to rejoice. The Lord has given us this day to live and to serve him and be glad.

Chapter Two

YOU NEED TO STAND

Exodus14:14 (NIV) The Lord will fight for you, "You need to stand."

It was very late Saturday night, I hadn't concluded my message for Sunday morning on Our Mission Corner. As I looked through my files at testimonies, I encountered a message that touch my spirit when I read the title and read the scripture. I said to myself, this is more than approval for my sermon, this is about me and my prevailing journey and what it may involve. Perhaps, I am wavering on some issues, I'll need to capture that weakness through more time with the Lord. The Lord doesn't want us wavering and teetering with every wave of emotion that will cause us to weaken our faith.

The Lord is very firm about his Word and what is will do for the believer. We don't need to chase other winds and doctrine, "You need to

Stand." The Lord says, reflect on pass experiences, witnessing, and testimonies. Many other factions will change, but not my Word.

Sunday morning, I met with the un-churched brothers; we had service where the spirit was in our midst, the Holy Spirit was upon His Word and we had words of agreement with us who was presence and were blessed by the awesome presence of the Holy Ghost and the word of God went forward. After the sermon had been preached, there were a feeling of fulfillment and needs had been met. I offer the right hand of fellowship to all that were presence, whether they had turned away from the Lord and want to return, you are welcome and those who have never received Christ as their Savior. I invited each of them to commit their lives to the Lord. One of the men that comes often, stepped up and said he wanted to give his life to Lord.

Early this morning, I had discomforts with my health, I am continually working on them through prayer and change of eating habits and visiting my doctor. I received a call from my sister, Prophetess Frankie, a powerful woman of

God, she tells me the spirit gave her a word for me, to pray and cancel all things that is evil and isn't of God. When we had finished praying, she said good bye without any conversation and I gave thought, who was this for? In a few minutes, I began to realize I had a dream early this morning and were concerned and needed to apply more effort to my health issue, but the Holy Spirit sent a word that cancelled any negative situation that blessed me beyond words. The Lord new I would need to stand, and He would fight for me. I felt His presence, to God be the glory and all praise go up to Him.

When we are even healing; overcomers being strengthen, if we are not careful, the enemy comes in and reverses things, steals your joy, takes away your courage, and leaves us feeling defeated. Because of our faith, the Lord sends witnesses and testimonies to what you heard that you can believe it is from our Lord, the Most High.

TRANSLATION: EXODUS 14:14 (NIV)

Moses called upon God to intervene. We may not be chased by an army, but we may still be trapped. Instead of giving into despair, we should adopt the attitude of Moses to" stand firm and see the deliverance of God.

Chapter Three

DECLARE THE WORKS OF GOD

Psalm 118:17(NIV): I shall not die but live and will proclaim what the Lord has done.

Job 42:10 (NIV) After Job had prayed for his friends, the Lord made him prosperous again and gave him twice as much as he had before. I felt the unction of the Holy Spirit very strongly when I read this. I am not certain all its mean. I received this the first time 14.47 on 1/22/11 and again on 11:28 am 06/22/19, His presence brought me to tears when I read the scripture.

I Peter 1:24 (NIV) "He himself bore our sins" in his body on the cross, so that we might die to sins and live for righteousness: by His wounds you have been healed.

Over the years when reading scripture, the written

word of the Lord, often gave me scripture and verses that were meant for me. Sometimes it was words of encouragement and other times it was for discipline, with directions or introduction towards works to come.

Sunday morning at the community church I read this scripture on Job 42:10 and late Sunday evening I were in my swimming pool, I were reading a study book on Angels, by Terry Law when I read this statement and were drawing into tears very strongly. The writer's states," He said," young man, I see a vision. God has called you, and He is going to send you around the world to preach the gospel. I see crowds of thousands and hundreds of thousands." On this time and date, I read this: 19:00 Sunday afternoon on January 12, 2011.

TRANSALATION: Psalm 118:17 (NIV)

There are days when the last thing we want to do is rejoice. Our mood is down, our situation is out of hand, and our sorrow or guilt is over whelming. We can be honest with God, tell God all about our troubles, and as we talked to him, our prayers end up in praise. When you don't feel like rejoicing, tell God how you truly feel. You will find that God will give you a reason to rejoice. God has given us this day to serve him gladly.

Chapter Four

PRAISE HIM

I Chronicles 4:10 (NIV) Oh, that you would bless me and enlarge my territory! Let your hand be with me and keep me from harm so that I will be free from pain," And God granted his request.

There have been tremendous prayers that have gone out and we are continuing to lay at the feet of the Lord for my health and strength as I continue in my storms, I am mindful and thankful that I am not alone in my battles for full recovery.

If we are listening, we can hear a word from the Lord when we have prayed for a word that will give us hope and build our confidence.

In August my pastor was preaching, in his sermon he said the only way someone would get what they stood in need of would be through the Lord. I felt the unction of the Holy Spirit when that was said I knew that was a word for me. Before I heard that sermon, early one morning a few days before, I woke, humming a few words that lifted me tremendously, that allowed me to be energized and become hopeful. The voice said, "I am healing you, He is worthy," a few days later on a Sunday night, I hear "Praise Him,"

Perhaps two weeks later, I hear one morning very clearly and friendly, "I'm going to heal you." I may have said something like, my Lord thank you and sent up praises, bless your Holy name, this is the second time I had heard this. I had been singing and humming those notes ever since I heard them. I received further support, again early in the morning, I awake singing, I look high, I look low, I can't find know body like you, a few days later I hear that in a song and added it to my previous support from the Lord Jesus Christ.

Lord Jesus gave me my song a few years ago, "I Surrender All," this is us, "offering ourselves to God," Roman 6:13, I realized there is a message in this song, I am trying to feel certain that I have committed myself completely to the Lord. I look at my chastisement for getting in wrong conversation and over a comment or don't agree with a response and speak to much about situations and circumstances. With those kinds of chastisements, came this word, "Create in me a clean heart, O' God and renew a right spirit within me."

I hear another beautiful but powerful song in my spirit one morning, now I realized I must be very careful, prayerful on wrong engagement in my conversation and that the Lord isn't please with me. This song comes early one morning, "I give myself away, so you can use me," on hearing myself clearly after I woke up, I am somewhat disturbed, so I asked myself, what did I fail to commit to the Holy Spirit? Now I am overly cautious in my conversation with others, I am fearfully when I fail to do what is right, because the Holy Spirit is righteous, and he brings it before us to get it right.

I am going through my issues on this journey prayerfully, led by the Holy Spirit to do other works on mission fields abroad and help bring the gospel of Jesus Christ to the unchurch. I am pending my journals, that it may help someone else on their walk with the Holy Spirit, that it is a serious task to be that which the Holy Spirit has called us to be. I thank the Lord every day for allowing me to be a servant of the, "Most High God."

TRANSLATION: *I Chronicles 4:10 (NIV)*

Jabez is remembered for a prayer request, in his prayer, he asked God to bless him, help him in his work and to enlarge his territory, be with him in all he did and keep him from evil and harm. He acknowledged God as the true center of his life. When we pray for God blessing, we should also pray that he will take his rightful position as Lord over our work, our family time, and our recreation. Obeying him in daily responsibilities is heroic living.

Chapter Five

LEARNING OBEDIENCE

Luke 9:62 (NIV) Jesus replied, "No one who puts his hand to the plow and look back is fit for service in the kingdom of God.

Early this morning, the prayer team were intercessors for others, and there were praise reports that went out, we were thankful to the Lord for answered prayers. He is the reason we come with prayer request, we bring all before the Lord. We crowd the heavens with our cries, with praises because our Lord is the answer.

Our Evangelist was prophetic, and spoke to our expectancy for 2011 with the move of the Lord, moving in the midst of our team we can expect assignments trends to lead us to increase our study of the scripture, increase in prayer and fasting. As our Evangelist prophesy, I made notes, I am frightened when I hear prophesy coming from the Lord, through his Evangelist. The Lord gave her a word to establish a prayer line in 2002 and it has been a powerful blessing through many years to many people, even today in 2018.

She always speaks with authority, as if the very words are coming from on High, from the mouth of the Lord, "You are the apple of my eye," I was very surprise to hear that on our prayer time. She goes on to say, He sees a pillar in you, you are to stay energized. Places to go, keep a full tank and be ready to go for Him. Servants are those who say yes to the Lord Jesus Christ and is willing to trust Him.

He leads us and covers us on our going out and coming in. Receiving that from the Evangelist were complete, because I had read it in the scriptures while reading and was convicted to tears in Zechariah 3:8. "Hear now, O Joshua the high priest, thou, and thy fellows that sit before thee: for they are men wondered at: for behold, I will bring forth my servant the, "Branch."

I said in my spirit, I am the guy, that didn't yield to his calling for many years. I finally said yes, I was in my early sixties. Our Evangelist gave me one off her favorite scriptures to support me and help me stay encouraged. "Trust in the Lord with all thine heart; and lean not unto thine own understanding. In all thy ways acknowledge him, and he shall direct your paths." Proverb 3:5-6.

TRANSLATION: *Luke 9:62 (NIV)*

No one can do any business in a proper manner, if he is attending to other things. Those who begin with the work of God, must resolve to go on, or they will make nothing of it. Looking back, leads to drawing back, and drawing back is to perdition. He only that endures to the end shall be saved.

ABOUT THE AUTHOR

Rev. Oscar Dixon

I was born in Roba, Alabama, August 29, 1942 to Ethel and Rev. Frank D. Dixon, he was a pastor in the Alabama A. M. E. Zion Church Conference. I gave my life to Christ at a very early age, about ten or eleven years old, and were baptized and joined The County Line A. M. E. Zion Church, under the pastorate of Reverend Robert Day.

Through prayer and fasting, I learned, I was called into the ministry at the tender age of fourteen by our Lord, Jesus Christ. As I grew up, I had many encounters from my youth to adulthood, my parents, explained these events, and finally they said we were peculiar children.

I am married, to Mrs. Gloria Allen Dixon, for over 56 years with two children, Oscar Lee and Melinda Rae Dixon

Chapman. We are grandparents to Oscar Najee and Natosha Dixon Porter, who gives us two great grands, Imani and Zechariah. When the Lord called me this time, he got my attention, I had retired from my job, and was in my late fifties. I had built houses and was renovating properties. Doing this time, I became very sick and, I didn't feel so deserving, but the Lord turned my fears into joy. My church family new of my struggles with my health and they prayed without ceasing, I remember my pastor saying to me, "Brother Oscar we are praying for you."

While working on my property, the Lord called my name, He asked me "Will You Serve Me," I said yes, and I have not looked back, but sought every opportunity to prepare myself to be able to serve. I took my theology studies from Beacon University, Columbus, Georgia, I achieved my Associate Degree, and Bachelors Degree of Theology. From the Christian Life Studies of Theology, I achieved my Master's Degree of Theology in 2013 and my Master's Degree of Sacred Studies 2019. I have three years in The African Methodist Episcopal Zion Church studies.

In 2005, I was invited to come on a mission trip into downtown Atlanta, I am still here working in 2017. I volunteered to work in two health and rehabilitation facility,

I began in 2007 and 2008. There is a take away in this spiritual focus, remember when you pray, believe what you have prayed for, and receive it as though it has already manifested itself, because The Lord answers prayers.

www.ingramcontent.com/pod-product-compliance
Lightning Source LLC
Chambersburg PA
CBHW030142170426
43199CB00008B/174